SOME MOTHERS' SONS

Charles Plymell

[signature: Charles Plymell]

Cherry Valley Editions
2004

Some Mothers' Sons

Library of Congress Cataloging-in-Publication Data

Plymell, Charles.
Some mothers' sons / Charles Plymell.
p. cm.
ISBN 0-916156-93-1 (pbk.)
I. Title.
PS3566.L95S66 2004
811'.54—dc22
2004000246

Cherry Valley Editions
PO Box 303
Cherry Valley, NY 13320

For those who take care
of the innocent creatures

For Robert Peters-
In his 80th year
of greatness

4

Charles Plymell, "Going to Kansas City", 1952

Cool Hobohemian's 1950's Bennies From Heaven

Sam Shusterman, the shoe store man, under the overpass and over the manholes in old downtown updone Wichita, has like a cast iron front store you'd see like on the Bowery. He sold dem used shoes to da old folk, poor folks and dos hipsters bopping down de street on Douglas Avenue, main drag, hip to de tip, a few blocks from the Great White Way Snooker Hall -- long time gone. He gots da used shoe store where da Florsheims shines and da floor shines too. He gots the time and da Togs to climb any gamey frame. He gots da Wingtips, hightops, blues suedes too. Off-size, replete, repaired, recast, retread, rebuffed, runover, factory rejects for da dejected, rejected, the prejudged multitude, da crude, da recluse, da dolly moppers and be-boppers, and suburb sinners at the door.

He stretches da off size, puts Scholls's in da too-wides. Black and white shoes for blacks and whites too. Pointy toes too for dos wid a point of view, pegged pachuco trousers, with silver watch-chained deja vu, oxfords for da saddle or da golf goof of course, even penny loafers for a memory of swing.

High heeled boots for shit stompers and whammied out galloping sluts. Hip boots laced in place, glittering fast socks clean up da alley cooch. Plastic pumps wid taps on de heels, patent leather for da patch pond n' gators galore.

I'm going down to Sam Shusterman's store across the Santa Fe tracks and get me something to bop the night train in, rack back my sack and lay my nod in da the bog before da sod, so fonk it and honk it, and trim the slim trinket 'cause I gots my new used kickers on, shufflin' and scufflin' down the street swift as a sneaker's shoestring, long time before Doc Martin made the scene.

6

Charles Plymell, Street Shot for a Dollar, 1952

WICHITA

Rapid Ronnie Rap Back Jive-Kansas 1955

Doc Moonlight bought a brand new T-bird from writing scripts
Amphetamines drove fast hard bodies over the high steppes
Fifty year' ago his daddy bought a mare in Dodge City
Wyatt Earp's grandson now sells new cars in Wichititty

Life on the high plains, borrowed on a pile of loans,
I drove; Ronnie handed me Pound's Selected Poems.
Outside Zip's Club we smoked and pissed
inside, Pack Rat picked his bass in bliss
his eyes rolled back, in closed fret
scoo bop to do, de bip bip, from hep
to hip, to hop, be de bop . . . next set
like cat cartoon characters boing back.
Swiinnging man, on an astrological star
his nose inhalers packed behind the bar
candy-wrapper's cosmos and benzedrine
dragnet, luncheonette, make the scene,
play it straight, if fate . . . says best
really bad, half sad, oh fay, oh say,
shuffle on down slide away from the mass
wanna smiz zoke a jiz zoint of griz zass?
Rapid Robert Ronnie Rasmutin Rannamuck

Thief, pimp, artist, hood
alias Barbital Bob—stood
under the neon of Zip's Club.
His subterranean bellhop's boyhood forays
met Kansas Big Intersection's wild mores.
By light from the stained glass windows
he sketched pictures between the shows.
Illuminated in gold-faced fading stories
he saw his dreams flyspecked with glory.
He stuffed his pockets with dope and dates of whores
while he gazed too far beyond the gayly painted doors.

Rapid Ronnie rides the moonlight high
Pack Rat scoffed pills and played melodic
drank Oxybiotic that made him neurotic
Jimmy Mammy, just outta the joint, heard
Big Indian was gonna steal Doc's Thunderbird.

Ronnie went along, reciting Pound's verse
riding the terrible crossroads of the universe.

Big Indian let out a yell of centuries of pain
drove into the Bulldog's tractor-trailer lane.
Jimmy Mammy broke his jaw and lay in years of highs
Ronnie grew old and secret under California skies.

Big Indian lay dead, his eyes confused
staring at the heavens . . . forever wider
than his moon's new earth that refused
him shelter from the great white spider.

Photo of Branaman and son at the beginning scene of "The Doors " © Branaman

*Robert Branaman married Sue Mack, debutante of Los Angeles. (Mack
Trucks/ Bulldog hood ornaments). In San Francisco they were intimates of
Billy Jharmark (Billy Batman/ Batman Gallery) and others of the 60's S.F.
Renaissance. They lived in Big Sur and at one time in a '52 Chevy on the
streets of S.F. They had three children. His son, an actor, first appeared
with Robert and his paintings in a cameo in The Doors movie. His older
daughter became a leading fashion model in L.A. Susan died of cancer at
an early age.

Charles Plymell, Kansas 1953, in 1952 Roadmaster Riviera bought in Hollywood

WICHITA

Allen Ginsberg and Neal Cassady in front of 1403 Gough St, S.F.,1963 taken by
Charles Plymell. Photo recovered from underground German magazine. No print
exists.

SAN FRANSISCO 1963
with Allen G. & Cassady

At the corner of Post St, and Gough
a chinaman had a store once called
the Golden West Market.

The government plans to tear it down.
They're crooks he says.
Where I flind another place for store?

At 1403 Gough St. there is a flat
which has stored past lives
in old baggage left by those
who saw too far behind
that pearly painted door.

Neal now
feverishly unloading old boxes
of clothes, books, belts, and tapes.
Carrying Anne across the threshold
where in the 50's LaVigne painted
Orlovsky's Superman man.

Allen returns to Gough St.
as saintly now as ever
Chaplinesque down the sidewalk.

You bring some tapes of
Ezra, and I recall an
eagle's eye wrinkled in stone.

That sculptured old man
alone with his muse.
Clarity of light years
wrecked in focused glory
of the unfit and unbroken.
Pound is still alive,
he's eighty-two you say.
Then you run around the
corner, your hair bouncing up and down.

The pawnbroker
of all unredeemed problems
of the worst of all possible worlds.
And I recall your gentle ways
when many lives were crossed upon
and set in mind of thee.

And the young burst forth untended;
blazing trails in long limousines.

Long-haired boys run past the house,
to the Avalon Ballroom scenes.

Popping their eternity
they run past the door

their rock and roll boots
more run over than before.
Past the '52 MGTD Classic
Billy Batman Jharmark just gave me.
Reality came from comics so fast that
Zap was coming soon, Like Jesus, Oh Janis
and some Rock n' Roll like you never heard.

When the Doors flung open in space, whirling,
hey man, when you're way out there alone
doing the old hip bop twist, reaching for the stars
Big Brother with Barbital Bob in Big Sur.

The back door by the tumbling stairs
where Neal returned years later, gone
in the face, Glenn said.
(Elephants, when ready, go
to their burial place.)
Where sister Betty and mulatto Frank from Deadwood,
son of an Irish sheriff and black madam slept off
cold Ripple nightmares' chemical wine
a slim thread of home to them all.
Maggie's wash now flaps between
the tree and dark lawn where cold
clouds crash, eclipse, churn
high above the jeweled ships
where suburban housewives' orange peels
go insane among coffee grounds and bones.

Crawling to the door's drag end
where choppy sea and fog take down
the sails of unrest, and throw a torch of amber ghosts.

Phil Whalen, Bob Branaman, Gary Goodrow, Allen Ginsberg, Bob Kaufman, Larry Ferlinghetti, Alan Russo, Charles Plymell, at City Lights Bookstore, San Francisco, 1963

Neal Cassady, Charles Plymell, outside 1403 Gough Street, S.F.,1963. Plymell sits on the first Honda import. Reproduction from magazine, no print exists

SONG FOR NEAL CASSADY

For John Cassady

Oh really really Neal
his first love was the automobile

Drove a '34 Ford with suicide doors
    and stick shift on the floor
        Draggin' down main to Colfax Avenue

Jumpin' in the back seat boulevard
    kicked back watching asses in the rearview
    cruising past the high school

Clock on the dash reading 10:18
past the neon diner
    last stop for Benzedrine
    and onward to another scene

Chicks would rob a joint
    just to buy him food

One hand on the wheel
    the other in her mood

The blue-eyed kid and the wild-eyed bobby soxer
    California surfers Tarot card sharks and word shooters

Found Ann-Marie in Frisco like a hurricane cock
    didn't need the Sexual Freedom League

Driving with white pills and pot
    but was really addicted to the wheel

Came back to Old San Francisco
    Flower children all over the streets

Carried star struck Ann-Marie in his arms
    the Denver Kid he never returns

Traded her Chevrolet coupé
    for an old Pontiac

Up the hills, down the curves
    gear it down, pump the brakes

Old mother Ginsberg's back seat drivin'
    turning toward the Avalon

Driving
    down Van Ness jumping parking meters

One hand on the gearshift
    the other copping a feel

One hand up her dress
    the other on the wheel

Stole a car in Denver just to hear it peel
    just like drivin' in the races

Stole a car in Denver just to hear it squeal

He moved so fast
    he had one foot in Cincinnati the other in Kalamazoo

Women knew just what to do
    and all wanted him to be true

Parked in front of Gough Street
    in a 50's red and white Plymouth Fury

Just back from seeing Kerouac, in a hurry
    patrol car in the mirror
    the old white and blacks

Drove past someone with some little white pills
    heading into town

He jumped in the driver's seat
    and spun that Fury around.

The roads were paved with powder all the way to Mexico
     and train tracks shined in the moon

Did hard time for two reefers
     and came out smokin' some boo

First Road Warrior
     never knew what he did wrong to

Neal Cassady and Anne Murphy, 1963, photo by CP, reprinted
from magazine.

Ray Bremser and Charles Plymell at Plymell's house, Cherry Valley Festival.
1998. S. Clay Wilson artwork on walls. © Catfish McDaris

NOVEMBER 3, 1998 DARK AFTERNOON

November,
and the clouds are heavy metal
rolling o'er the vacant brick of Utica
where Ray lies in his death throes
at the Faxton Cancer Hospital.

It's not a happy sight, a
finality about the rooms and service
his roommate's exposed privates
both he and Ray seem far away.

In and out of sensed reality
I fear to say, eyes like animals in cages

Ray's eyes sometimes intense
screaming "I want to die"
not in a philosophical mode
but the growl used for prison guards

rattling his bones against the
iron bars of New Jersey.

Squirts of daylight on the sidewalk
like used rubber gloves thrown
among the slimy Autumn leaves
Study the sight, oh latter night Beats.

Another is passing into the night
like T.V. tonight Jimmy Smit
on NYPD the line of fictive reality
unto death, what to do with life's purpose?
If it's to understand life (loved the old comedies)
from those eyes just make ourselves over
Ray watch the old realities in black and white
He pulls on the bed rails : "I want to die."
His eyebrows move and he briefly conducts
a conversation he can't partake in
or a Katchaturian concert or a poem.
He leans back, eyes glazed, goes elsewhere
further than shooting up decades ago
the history gone like our rides for Terpinhydrate
finding village drugstores while the world went on.

What history can a human have? The history gone
the religions, the politics, the last fiction...not that
faith, miracles, and belief isn't real
there's just never enough to go around.

Don't tell me his spirit has to hitch a ride
'round about midnight'
to make a visitation when the sky
rolled back its spheres to let the gold sun
wail like a sax over the stage of East Hill
for an original hipbeatster camping at
the Committee on Poetry farm
where he said he used to talk more shit
than the radio which he didn't own.

TOKEN FOR BEAT HIP STREETCAR CAT
HOBOHEMIAN BREMSER FROM HOBOKEN

(From the tongue of the Mahican to the Nanticoke for towns in New Jersey)

I have gone to Manasquan
left at dawn from Matawan

Got to go past Hopatcong
or that away to Piscataway

Totowa or Ho Ho Cus

That you ahawkin'
in Manahawkin
or talkin broken in Hoboken

Weehawken all the way
to Wanaque and Succasunna
do you wanna
Secaucus all around Moonachie

Photo © Laki Vazakas, 1998

Ray Bremser was one of the original, if not one of the most authentic Beats, a hipster from the same vein as Herbert Huncke (probably closest to him philosophically than others), from the jazz subterranean world down the block to where Kerouac was blowin'. He lived a spartan lifestyle (not without excesses) associated with the early Beat movement. A bed on the floor in a room a couple times bigger than a cell, a few tattered books and a sink to piss in was home to him. He was not a clean liver by any means. His pad was probably more like Howard Hughes's, except in Ray's case filled with labyrinthian mounds of beer bottles, cans and ash trays.

His economics were similar to Huncke's, too. Always on the hustle, scuffling enough for beer, cigarettes, drugs, and a room. He had one windfall from a class-action suit against the state, which brought several thousand to his kitchen table piled high with butts and beer cans and thousands of dollars. He lived in a pad in Utica with no street numbers. I talked to a couple of black guys at the door to find him. He gave me a thousand to go for cigarettes, saying to keep the change and not to say he ever owed me anything. He went through the thousands in one day.

He loved experimental prosody, had a gift for gab; his loquacity and sarcastic tone added a beautiful bass to his New Jersey accent; he liked to jive and put people on. He said he "talked more shit than the radio." Always laughing or snickering, mostly caustic, his religious motives more satirical than serious. His poetry had the same jazz, surrealist, existential, hip tones as did his "street-beat" contemporaries, Jack Micheline and Bob Kaufman. Though unlike Kaufman, social and political agendas didn't prevail, but set a tonal backbeat which made his linguistic experiments cohere or "work" in the sense that Jackson Pollack coined. He demanded from the listener, which sometimes caused unenlightened reporters to miss the poetry. His voice was of New Jersey, a proletariat east chemical coast flatlander. "What Hoboken Makes, the World Uses", he used to recite the sign for the prophylatic industry in his home town.

Rod McKuen and Charles Plymell at Edgar Allen Poe Gravesite, Baltimore, 1976

Life is a poor host grabbing guests who came
swirling great pleated sheets wrapping the stars
leaving, streaming party coils to their last cars
some on twilight's slightly twisted cane.

From Charles Plymell's poem "Was Poe Afraid", *Hand on the Doorknob*,
Water Row Press, 2000

AT ROD'S READING IN TIMES SQUARE, 2001

She ran into his dressing room happily shouting
she may as well have died and gone to heaven
her young relative, embarrassed, apologetic
having driven her from nearby state and town
what else could Rod do but hug her
and say he'd go to heaven with her

How jealous can we poets be to have fans like that?
She said she had waited a lifetime for this moment.

The Chinese carry-out down the street, the
Japanese restaurant in neon glow, adrenaline flows
outside the glitter voltage rises around Rod's name
on the marquee, in Times Square, the new electric glitz
now emanating from the B. B. King Club where
Rod sits perched on the familiar stool on stage:
an ideogram becoming word and symbol one

The mike, the stool, the stage and perched leg
at the first or second rung, a symbol he's become
his songs yet more lyrical, his gift more seasoned
the poet's world has changed after all, and all of us
may be orphan'd like the stars in too vast of space

Whatever minds have conceived to help our plight
it is universal that love is the most powerful force
and the song has always been the abstraction of it
beyond all and many variables in the human walk of life
The heart and voice are one, from the tattoo parlor
a few doors down 42nd St, to tattooed constellations
ancients pierced forever in stars of the night sky, a
singer, a creature of that steady prosody will sense

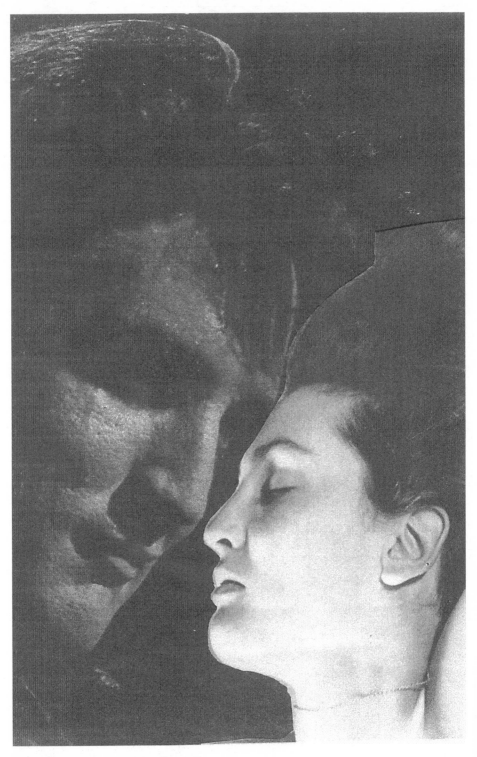

Collage by Charles Plymell

"Can you hear the sound of the breaker sliding under the collage-
guy's cutter? *Time* is the only LAW."

Claude Pélieu

IMAGIST

At Claude Pélieu's funeral service Norwich, NY, Dec 30, 2002

We lived the good times, those years, Chano Pozo
and all that jazz . And I know why you preferred
the land of many icons, art and faces changing like
old forms tearing from images that float in space
tonight as we drive to your improbable resting place
while the pewter clouds obscure the pearlish sun
playing behind the dark hills, floating French drapes
never seen before, casts forever aurora eyes in the wings.

CUT PRAISES

At William Burroughs' funeral service Lawrence, KS, Aug. 6, 1997

The Muse is satiated, well paid
Her splayed wand, still sparking
Her stray cats all found a pillow
Her Nefarious boy came home
Osiris, share thy Throne

Paul Bley, Charles Plymell, David Greenspan, Bill Heine, at Jamie and Jeremiah's house, Cherry Valley, 2003 © Laki Vazakas

"My Buddy" In a Cardigan Sweater and Axe in the Back Seat.

Chatting on a snowy night in Cherry Valley in a little building where Samuel Morse sent his first telegraph message and some old tickers still hang on the wall and the grand piano takes up the rest of the room. Top floor sags with boxes of recordings of every jazz musician known. Paul played with them all and tonight throws another log on the fire, each flame spurs a new note of memory. He commutes to Europe to play his gigs. Why don't you play here at universities? Much simpler than flying all over the world? Like every question, a story of experience follows. They know me over there. Same people expect me every year. The deal is always up front, everything taken care of. Don't have to ask. Whatever stuff and money I need the guy knows and hands it to me as I go on stage. It's all like improvisational, gig and all. I chat a while, enjoy the best each country has to offer, go to bed and fly home. Here, I have to jog with some kid from the Student Union, who then has to put it before the committee. I have to jog with him, eat a campus pizza or hot dog and then he says he'll let me know what the committee decides. And the honorarium might be in the mail after the next budget meeting. The next year someone new handles the gig. They've likely never heard me. They're a music industry major. It's a long trip, but I'd rather fly than jog.

He had a story for anyone I'd name through the century like high-lighting the Montreal festival with Chet Baker who went on the nod at the last minute and Paul had to do the whole number. Getting sick after playing for Lucille Ball in the 50's who took him to the hospital and stayed with him until he was well.

I asked him to put all this in a book like Blake said, so that all may read. Same with Charles Henri Ford. I took Paul to meet him at the Dakota. Living histories. Who needs Liberal Arts? Paul's book is titled, *Stopping Time*. Charles Henri's is called *Water from a Bucket*. If one wants an education, invest college tuition in the tech market in India and buy these books and a few others. Sit by the fire with Paul, don't ask him to play though, because everything is an improvisation and any improvisation is a concert, but any con-versation is enlightening. We wandered up to Ginsberg's old farm-house. An old pedal organ was in the corner. Paul did a concert for three. At Jamie's party in Cherry Valley Bill Heine came up from Woodstock. He wanted to know who the guy was in the living room. He went to sit with him. It turns out they both played with Charley Parker in the 50's.

The telegraphic space stayed humming. Cool, live, relaxed. Laki recording in time. My dog named Bebop lay at their feet. The story gig got going like jam, jam, jam session long ago with a Buick convertible loitering against a Harlem curb. Lucky Strike red wrap-per, Pennsylvania Hotel, black LaSalle, neon tapestry session all connected over the years. The squares will go about their lessons, jogging in the exhaust of Firebirds in yet another century and in yet another unseen night on the Great Western Turnpike, my buddy, the keyboard man can tell you.

Plymell at Ford's Ubu Gallery opening, NYC, May 20, 1999, © Gerard Malanga

CHARLES HENRI FORD'S LAST PRINTS

Atlas on this star-studded Montauk
Beach, bleached night of dead cartilage
rotting haunting puzzles to their core.
Straddle night's space glazed with numbered
stars each to each pebble on the shore.

If you stand and throw your great knife
and cut an imaginary line through the
night sky, it is said that space is
so vast that no star would be hit.

Surrealism's magic master, beachcomber, leaves
lines like Spiderman's spit on skyscrapers
Gotham's duo, Batman, Robin and the rest.
Where Montauk descendants sell tobacco.
Leave your signals for a physicist to predict
and keyboard specialist to plunder the growing
algebraic garden of poppies, not having heard
such names as Tanguy, or Charles Henri, who,
before computers, had seen fractal patterns
curl back upon themselves as clean and easy
as a cut through space, a thread in Persian rugs,
or Seahorse dance in pride from deep ocean's ridge.

The course lives in the dance, in footprints, or
in the throne of worlds, the gnomon, Osiris sits upon.
Myth and geometry meet in the mouth and in the maw,
or in carcass washed ashore where upon he sits in
quick poppy's charm, in the kitchen's lost creations
raw food in the salons now gone, no more fine blade
slicing symmetry of the seed, or chopping herbs.
Latex oozing from the night, like a field of
Milky Way's frozen eternal footsteps above 72nd St.

The space time sung anew, like the canaries do, and
be bop too, to save their memories' weight for flight.
The brain lightens and ideas are boats untied
left in the currents of neurons,
less fantasized postulates school kids study
while long bladed orbits assassinate lovers
when the bare-light bulb moon dims the sun's room
unexplained, resonating, unscrewed, unfurnished with
the future by transient vestal vacancies of the past.
Sing for us, play for us, pray for our minimalist souls
while we sit in Acuras watching manipulators
coasting in Manhattan on roller blades of black ice.

Ford's 94th birthday party, © Grant Hart

William Burroughs, Charles Plymell, James Grauerholz , Lawrence, KS.

Last Days of The Generation

I was unnoticed at the university ballroom in that dusty old cowboy town that the James Gang would make as famous as Rodeo Drive. I was in the long lines waiting for autographs by Bill and Allen until Pat O'Connor told them I was there.

They immediately put me at the table between them, and some of the people in line shifted to have me sign whatever they had. One pushed a dollar bill in front of B. He looked at it, turned it over poker-faced and silently shoved it back to the person. Later, we went over to the famous little Sears Roebuck cottage for the last meal these two principal beats would have together.

We had to go shopping for G. who spent most of the dinner talking about his diet, how he avoided sugar. They both were asked on stage that day, what was their favorite line in all literature. B said, "Tomorrow, tomorrow, tomorrow", and A. said "That in black ink my love may still shine bright." After dinner, he tried to remember some preceding lines. I told him it was easier to start at the beginning of the sonnet, and I began reciting the whole thing. Like in a grade B cowboy movie where the outlaw tires of the Shakespeare player, B started fingering his .38. James put his hand on his shoulder as if to say, let him finish, which I did, showing off.

Soon the Kansas moon was up. B was prowling in his pyjamas. James and I stood standing under a cottonwood. We came back in. A. was offered some desert and remind us that he didn't eat sugar. B was passing around the famous skull carved in Mexico from sugar. I quipped, "At least Allen won't eat your skull!" I got a chuckle from Burroughs, who said, "No, Ginsberg won't eat my skull."

Dangerous Dan, Cherry Valley, NY Photo © William Plymell

Dangerous Dan

Down Gooney Lane onto the dork dark morning Main
Onto the highway lane in the rain nobody looked too sane
Dangerous Dan, he's the man, lived in a van and had the plan
To go to the city to the great Comix show to see his hero
Gonna be trippy for the world's last hippy to see the Checkered Demon
drink from Tree Frog beer can for a clan of pirates and demon fans.
Dangerous Dan lived down the holler where the pussy willows grow.
Keeps afloat, ragged coat, jumped in the Caddy when
We all went down to the city to see the comix show
Drivin' in the rain passing everything that came in every lane
Driver ain't no slouch, has a pouch, drinks scotch, scratches his crotch
Three men and a dame packed in the back, three in front shooting film.
Line three blocks long standing in the rain, I spotted the artisan, Spain,
who got us in the packed gallery where we couldn't move body to body
From the back came Ginsy and Crumb. I asked where's Wilson
He's in the back signing autographs but you can't get to him.
Ginsy said to me gesturing to crowd, Look what you started a long time ago.
Sweating crowd dripping, couldn't breathe, left the show
Had to get some air in the streets of NYC, parked the Caddy at the nearest bar
Black man yelling in a toxic zone, head's in one world, heart's in another
Dan under the car in the gutter wiggling the drive shaft because of noise
Left the city in the rain speeding into New Jersey, driver out of his brain
Patrol car sirens blasting away, driver speed up to get away
Whole fleet of patrol on our tail, pulled over the Caddy next to a rail
Divers' license? Just in the process, driver handed him paperwork mess
Whut's this? Yr kindergarten report? Outta the car, hands over head!
One at a time. You next! Don't stand behind me! Stand in front!
Then out of the back seat Dan's turn. He stuffed his weed in his sock.
Troopers tore through the trunk, sure they had something, but what?
Any guns or knives. Dan being searched said No. Found his pocket knife
which all good mechanics carry to get the grease out of their fingernails.
WHAT'S THIS? The trooper yelled! Uh, my pocket knife, said Dan.
The troopers lined up in their laced boots and knee pants, knew they had
something here, but what? I was the last to get out. Old man with beard
and hippie head band. Look I said. We're from a small village upstate.
Wanted to have a night on the town, ya know, and it's hard to find a
driver in the boonies. They looked at each other, I heard 'em say low.
Think of the paperwork, better let 'em go. Twin towers in the skyline

Ray, the driver, obviously dying of something, guy in the passenger seat
with his baseball cap on backwards, too old, me too old, the Cadillac
too old for a limousine, the batman signal painted on the trunk.
Follow the signs for the New York Thruway. Get the hell outta
New Jersey and don't come back. We listen to the Caddy Radio
all the way home. How sweet the rock. How comfortable
the back seat. How near we'd been to the booking room and a
night in jail. Never got to see Wilson. A few years later in San Francisco
he told me someone told him I was at the Comix show and he came
from the signing in the back, shouting Plymell and everyone looked
at him like he wuz nuts. Wilson came to visit an Easter when it snowed.
The next winter Dan in band Carl Waldman put together at his house
Dangerous Dan on Drums, Carl on guitar and "Bad Veronica" the lead
singer who had black hair. And the Blonde ran away with the
Checkered Demon.

S. Clay Wilson, Dangerous Dan, 1997, Plymell house

Ray Bremser, Charles Plymell, Grant Hart, in front of the abandoned farmhouse in Cherry Valley, NY where Ginsberg and others lived during the "Committee on Poetry" years.

Photo by Betsy Kirschbaum, ©1998 Water Row Books. Used by permission.

FOR GRANT HART

How would the old homestead ever know
who would occupy its future centuries
Oh the maple farmer and his sleigh
Oh the bard and his harmonium
a cord of wood, a wicker rocker
a wolf-lipped greybeard poet then
the punk rock balladeer singing to the poets
past the songs that make you think

St. Paul kid named after the five & dime
Faces sunshine under the old porch roof that
never falls, just leans, though many snows have
blown upon its brim like a dream of a do-rag.

Where possum and mouse and cat lived many lives
with uncounted ants through the centuries'
hut entities, pot-honored, warmed the inner flesh near
snuggled old house basking winsome burdened wine
blues space bartered etched smoke from woodstove fire.

Grant, Ray, Janine and I now look into the hills like
we came to the carnival of 'round ladle rat rotten huts as
the centuries fall down on us, but the porch roof stays
wetter than last year's Mallard orphans swimming on the pond.

Cats scratch and dogs bark, and ticks battle lids under naked eyes
of the moon's inner florist above yonder sorghum stenches
memories stick resplendent on the Burdock cockles velcro
and no schedules are made for road gigs met just in time
for the singing and playing and music's arms
raised to the tune of the brooding century's bottle of beer.

Andy Clauson, Charles Plymell, Ray Bremser, Janine Pomy-Vega at the Cherry
Valley Festivlal. © Catfish McDaris

Charles Plymell at Bitter End, NYC, 1999, Photo © Levi Asher

Fable written and performed during the search for JFK Jr.'s airplane, July 19,1999

THE PRINCE OF TIDES

The King of the most powerful land was preparing his reign of peace, freedom, and equality for all his people. The Queen was preparing for birth of the new Prince. But there were problems. His armies were engaged in a conflict they could not win. The young did not want to fight the unknown enemies that the old had made to keep power. Much to the Queen's dismay, who was busy rearing the new Prince, the King had also fallen under the spell of the Sex Goddess who ruled in the Make Believe World.

In order to draw attention from his problems, he promised his people and the Goddess something impossible. The Moon was inviolate and pure through all the millenniums. It was the symbol of an untouched heavenly body. On a hot July day when the seas of the earth were hazy his spacemen set foot on the moon and played a sport. For beings from Earth, landing on the moon was the greatest of all feats, but other Heavenly Bodies grew angry and sent a tremor through space.

The others ordered the moon to multiply the earth beings until they poisoned themselves with their sciences, inventions, and technologies that they thought would better their race and protect themselves. The toxins made them act strangely and kill each other in inhuman and unpredictable ways. The other Heavenly Bodies also put a curse on the Sex Goddess who died mysteriously, reportedly taking her own life. The King was assassinated, his brain stolen, and the event so obscured that the Queen and her people would never know the truth. The toddler Prince saluted his father's horse-drawn casket. The king's brother was also assassinated and tragedy befell more of the family.

The Prince grew into the handsomest and most desired by all peoples. Even a Princess from another country came to visit him. The millennium was drawing to a close. Strange events happened more frequent. The Princess' great beauty was crushed by a new lifestyle of high-speed technology and metal. With his wife and sister by his side, the Prince flew his new sleek-wing'd technology into a July haze just a few years after the Queen had died. Before the new millennium, in the same month the King had made the moon his conquest, fabulous remains washed ashore in silent pieces where the Queen had once played with the child Prince while the King governed his people.

Charles Plymell and Thurston Moore, 2001, Photo © Gerard Malanga

Imaginary Typical Morning

Like my dreams when I fall back asleep
in the morning. Half-real cartoons play
themselves out, sometimes cluttered,
sometimes clueless, some pretty real
but nearly always, someone I know.

Imaginary, so long ago, when sunlit eyelids
saw the waning of their own stars though
someone has thoughtfully gone out for bagels.
The coffee brewing in the kitchen.

Mr. Malanga reads the newspaper at the table
Coco propped on a pillow in her chair in front of TV
watching cartoons characters bump in their mishap worlds of
innocent escapades and calm trivial chat and circumstance
that holds me in an imaginary universe of an imaginary universe
proposed by Dr. Hawking in an article at the edge of the table
and at the edge of another universe not really chosen;
the world is the way it is because it could not be otherwise.

Absurdity reigns in the TV innocent morning big kitchen
where everything is peaceful in the calm cartoons as I remember
picking up my daughter from her Lower Eastside daycare
long ago, take her to our Bowery loft to watch the calming Mr. Rogers
of the imaginary, imaginary world at the edge of the universe at Bowery.

Thurston toasted a bagel, teased Coco with grown up concepts
wife/mother abstracting from the TV imaginary universe to real life
Joined by Eileen and friend, Kim, Byron and others in what seemed
like a good all-American family scene that may not be really
our past scenes, which couldn't have been all that bad unless.....

Seen by beholder who sat in a half-warp on the edge of cartoons
with the extra-ordinary, extra-terrestrial, as I sat in an imaginary
world and let the birds in the branches outside the window think
about time in a universe that is in all time joined by a child
in myth and play beyond a window at the edge of a world
we knew before the cartoon turned to dark news of new century.

In the front yard of the Committee on Poetry farmhouse, Cherry Valley, NY, 1970, Gregory Corso, Anne Buchanan, Gordon Ball, Ed Yurich, Maretta G., Allen G., Rick, Allen and Joan DeLoach, Mary Beach, Miles, Claude Pelieu, Pam and Elizabeth Plymell, Charles Plymell, Ray Bremser, Bonnie Bremser, standing - Denise, Peter Orlovsky. © Allen DeLoach.

TREE SONG FOR ALLEN GINSBERG
                                April 5, 1997

Chirp, chirp, chirp
Ginzy gone
I broadcast the seeds
bread crumbs from the compost
for little animals and birds

Chirp on the phone, chirp on the radio
broadcasting them seeds
Janine left a message on the phone
I read it in chirp cyberspace

Up Lancaster St. we drove
past the bank on East Hill Road
New house where'd you come from
another house along this road

that one didn't used to be there
yet another on the way to the farm
that was the idea of a farm for poets, etc.

The great view of the Mohawk Valley
its early spring mauves and browns
old crops of gold fields stalks

Didn't take the shortcut where
Ray froze his fingers round a beer can
walking to Cherry Valley in a blizzard

Turn off the paved road
Bad hill bad ruts from spring washes
Peter needs to get that tractor
and haul some dirt and gravel

Like he usta with the manure spreader
Julius faithfully standing on the hitch
Big tractor at the corner
have to walk in here
Roads all wet, parts covered with snow

Hear the birds already
Get the bread pieces
throw a few
tie my shoe

Walk down the slushy ruts
through mud and snow
old craggily cherry tree
must be a hundred

You said the old ones were wiser

"Broadcast" the bread a metaphor
when you were born, tho most had radio
more bread for the bashful birds
Stop here to rest and share
my hard bagel with the birds
hmm. that doesn't taste bad
maybe I'll eat it meself.

Hardly a sound up here in hushed forest
the snow is silent in the deer tracks
Pam says the daffodils are in bloom

I'll put some bread crumbs on the porch
not on this chair with peeling paint
Bread on the old maple tree
bread on the rock for innocent creatures

A rag is hanging on the old clothesline
and the barn door needs repair
the whole barn actually, I'll leave
some crumbs by the outhouse and
the barn and the cherry tree

On the road back a woodpecker
breaks the silence, hammering perfectly
like a Whitman carpenter
Burdock sticks like Velcro
Bread on the windowsill
bread on the rock
Old truck rusting away
new tires rotted in place
never helped anyone
get anywhere or nowhere anymore.

The air always changes on East Hill
like the atmosphere of heavens
the stars come down to
a respectable level in
case you need to chat with 'em

It is heavy now and the sun is
burning like chrome in the grey sky
the woods are mauve and brown dark green
the green and grey neglected cottage
weathers by the green and grey pound
The mountains and the sky are all blue
various shades enshrouding the Evergreens
white birch arises from moss green rock
of old hills and forests

You walked me to the boundary
twenty-nine years ago
probably talking of Whitman and Death
Now you know
And I know
The Committee on Poetry is a bird,
a barn, a pond, a daffodil, an outhouse
And a silent cottage of memory rooms.

Charles Plymell, James Graureholtz, William Burroughs, John
Giorno at the Committee on Poetry pond, East Hill, NY,

46

Fred Douglass Plymell, in front of his father's house, Oklahoma Territory.

In Memory of My Father

To you who sung the riddles of that desolate Atlantis
while wind worn wagons swept a sunken trail into eternal dust.
To your sod, your grass, your easy hills of flint from glacial
slope to wanderlust. "Perfect cattle country . . . the best I've
seen since Uruguay." I'd oft heard you say, your dreams and maps
unfolded beneath those eyes that inventoried skies and knew
the winter owl's alarm where black beasts of Angus grazed?
I could not see as far, but went my way, you understood, and
watched the windmills tell their listless joy to silt and seam.
Life must be beautiful or all is lost . . . those bison of the clouds
were pushed from life . . . slaughtered for sport . . . now they are
the storm clouds watching us from eternity and far beyond.

And I did not know (when you showed me the lilies on the
limestone.) No . . . I did not notice you had grown old, your
hair had turned to silver . . . for I never thought you'd die.
I thought when this would end we'd all join hands together
like you told the babes at playtime long ago (that you hoped
we'd all meet in Heaven) in that dust bowl depression of Kansas.
It is hard to notice age in those who dream. You knew,
dreams are like youth, without them the world could not continue.
They are like the trees you always planted on sun-parched steppe,
enjoyed by those who pause and dream beneath the steel of time.
O fading America! Where is Thy promise! 0 catastrophic land!
This land you loved when newborn calf kicked up its legs . . .
you said everything wants to live . . . and expresses it.

The slap, slap, slap of tires on the grey concrete.
The tears on the way to the funeral. The biggest sky in Kansas.
"Wish I could find that old house where Grandmother lived,"
someone said, trying not to think, or feel, or sob.
You had told me you "might kick off" one of these days,
but I could never see you anywhere but waiting for us
on the porch, arms folded always with finger prop't
against sunburned cheek, Stetson tipped back, calm grey
eyes anxious and kind through smoke of neglected cigarette.
Home for Christmas in a few short days with newborn babe.
Giant cranes along the ditch . . . steel helmet'd
construction workers laying concrete pipe beyond all
of the Family Store T.G. & Y. or the old folks home you cussed.

Under vast space you saw the end products of wasted soul & hand
You saw the time begin to change, you saw the Atom Bomb.
You knew the true nature, foresaw the greed and plastic goods.
Saw those old jaws of monster oil wells pumping the never ending
depletion allowance of blood of man and earth.

"The little man pays the taxes."

And you sensed the vacant stare in faces. You saw man change.
You saw him buy on time. But he had no time to talk now. No time. No time.
Car tires squeal on nowhere road to make a time payment.

Skull of memory, how will your lamp burn now?
How will the dust, like pages scorch that canopy of bone?
How will those eyes rest against the dark storm of tears now,
when ozone rests on sage, calming that stampede of time?
It was the day of mustangs, the day a train whistle screamed that
Rockies' grade, when double header highballed and howled past
diesel trucks, water towers of unknown towns; soliloquy of
settlements and cemeteries beyond truck stops and salvage yard.

It was said you payed the ambulance driver before you let him go.
You dug some bills out of your old leather purse to hand him.
Through your hard span of life, you settled up so quietly
no one ever thought of you carefully.
They didn't care for unknown sages in unknown towns.
The end of a man, an age. I neglected to hug or kiss.

I was coming to see you from school, bringing my family.
Your father died with the fence unmended, the calves got out,
he didn't feel like riding; waited for you to come from school.
Everything changes but the meaning, and the tenderness passed on.
I stand here beside the peaceful grave, I stand here on earth
for the first time without you by me;
I take this land upon my shoulders.
The grain elevator over there is filled with wheat, the seed of
newborn day. The green Spring wheat. I am a father now. I know.
Your folks from Indiana came overland in covered wagons
crossed the Muddy at Hannibal Mo., Mark Twain was 36.
To Belle Plaine and on to "No Man's Land." You staked your

claim. I remember the joke about no birth certificate, and
how the neighbors were healthy because they had government jobs.
Charley Dumbell shot himself with a Colt .45. You told the kids
wild stories, listened to Joan Baez, your favorite, with teenage kids.
You were always young and built the fence for your daughter's horse.
Lifting beams bigger than railroad ties . . . against the doctor's orders.

Post hole diggers left in the holes of prairie sod never used again.

Fred Douglass Plymell, 1924

FROM ANCIENT LAND (Vernal Equinox Dream)
Washington, D.C. 1984

They walked the sunrise, soul-burned travelers,
wearing hats tilted like Autumn's landscaped hills.
Rough-faced sailors, eyes laden like water rills
scanned the horizon till shorelined stars unfurled.

New wind in the air for those waft on the seas,
new smell of earth dug away to align the leys*.
And they came forever wandering, as if set free
from cracks and rifts and vortices, as when some
great stone moves from its natural mortises; they
sailed the wind, a front of chaotic charges ignited,
careless in radiance, patterns of heaven unsighted.

(At 5:30 a.m. I awoke from a dream of Vernal Equinox
like a farmer called early for spring plowing, or a
driver with an early start knowing the aching miles
that stretch across the long heart of the prairie.)

In the Oklahoma Territory my father left his coffee pot
on the stove in his sod house, and he drove
cattle down to Galveston town. He saw the
lights beckoning on the port side of the bow,
headed for Italy, brought back a color picture
of the Isle of Capri, and when he returned the
next year, the coffee pot was in the same place.
And the picture for years was the only decor alone
in the farmhouse room askew from a rolling cyclone.
The wind, a terrible pitched-moan to stillness,
silent as trowels through the loess* and grass.
Blowing dust through cracks of doors and windows,
sculpted the still waves day and night. The house
took in the wind of the wolves' howl, the song
of the coyote, and the long train whistle dragging
the reptile's whispering scream of time; the pioneer's
pitch of desperation, first loud then soft as the crimson sun
then distant into the stars where cowboys herded
the dark clouds out of the sky and sailors lined
the bow like star bodies, wanderers, happily growing

visitors who come when the new wind comes to keep me half
awake, half dreaming. . .so very many
where deep chasms of history gives dazzling narrow light

My father rode down through the equinox in a perfect
visioned dream as if he had never been away. I
wanted to show him the nation's capital, but he
was here on other business; he wanted to find his
merchant marine papers, why, I don't know, maybe
to show passage through eternity beyond cold space.

'Look at the beautiful masonry,' I said to him, 'look at
the Merchant Marine Building with its exquisite work
of brick and tile, and bronze doors, and frontispieces.'
We went down to a little section of the city by the sea.
'Oh,' I said to him, 'this is just like Italy.' The marble
and the little streets and the glassworks and the women
who walked there, the women he joked with, and the sailors,
and the bricklayers, and the carpenters, and threshers
like Kansas long ago, drifters passed in the street
recognized in memory, composite in chirality, patient
in formality; they, the blazed-faced, hand-hewn people
who walked the narrow streets by outdoor cafes.

He knew where to go, not up to the marbled entrance
but down a side street low, near a building, where,
in the dust of the sea bottom, beneath a small cupola
stood a woman by a counter of endless floating files.

'Draw me a picture of the last scene you remember
as a mariner,' she said. He drew a picture of himself
sitting on a bed, his sailor's hat cocked to one
side, a coffee cup on the table. He asked her jokingly,
'how do you want me, ma'am, hobbled and ironed?'
She helped him look. 'How far back?' He didn't know.
Down in the sea dust of a bottom drawer they found
his papers water stained brown. He pulled them out
and waved and yelled as if he had found passage
toward the wild fix of stars, or Isle of Capri.

Notes: This memory poem came to me at around 5:30am at the time of the vernal equinox when we were living in Washington, DC. It turned out that Allen Ginsberg had a dream about his mother at that very same time, on the vernal equinox. His poem was later published in the New York Times. Another coincidence was that he was reading at American University a few nights after we had both written the poems. We went out to eat before I took to his room after his reading. I showed him the poem to my father and he made some minor editing marks on it and then told me about his dream about his mother and the poem he wrote for her.

* European Leys, archeological sites along astrological alignments perhaps tracing water holes and pagan rituals. Sometimes parts of gathered stones found in such places as Brittany. The author's forebears have been traced to a region near Ploermel, France.
* loess, fine glacial sediment found in Kansas.

Fred Douglass Plymell, Oklahoma Territory, beginning of Twentieth Century.

An Appreciation

Gerard Malanga

15 : I : 04

Dear Charlie,

I want to thank you for sharing with me this booklet of poems to your dad. I read the entire booklet outloud to myself to catch the nuances and twists & turns of your rhythm, like I was riding a stagecoach kicking up the dust and small stones along the way. No soft shoulders here. The years of tramping and riding rough have worn down the ground in spots I imagine.

These poems, like some others I read in *Hand on the Doorknob*, certainly evoke atmosphere and the sense of bygone days. The easygoing voice within you cradles these memories in a way I can imagine you rolling a smoke.

I look forward to reading more of the same as you wend your way back through your personal and very unique history.

Best regards,
Gerard

Back to Front: Catfish McDaris,Tom Deventi,Charles Plymell, Mary Beach, Herschel Silverman, Al Duffy, Alan Kirschbaum, Pam Plymell, Andy Clauson, Antoine Mahoney, Claude Pelieu, Micheal Buchenroth, Grant Hart, Ray Bremser, Jeff Weinberg, Dave Church, In front of Plymell's house, Cherry Valley Arts Festival, 1998.

A special thanks to all those who particitpated in the Cherry Valley Arts Festival. Especially Breath Hand for bringing it all together.

And a special thanks to Elizabeth Plymell for putting together this fine little collection. Fond memories all, Cherry Valley, '04.

Some Mothers' Sons may be ordered from:
Cherry Valley Editions
P.O. Box 303, Cherry Valley, NY 13320
cveds@nycap.rr.com

Price per book - $12.00
Shipping and Handling - $3.50

Front cover photo: Fred Douglass Plymell in the Merchant Marines, 1920's

Back cover photo: Charles Plymell, from the movie "Ephemeral Blues" by Wayne Sourbeer, 1954

Also by Charles Plymell

Past Titles

Apocalypse Rose, Dave Haselwood Books, San Francisco, CA, 1967.
Neon Poems, Atom Mind Publications, Syracuse, NY, 1970.
The Last of the Moccasins, City Lights Books, San Francisco, CA, 1971;
Moccasins Ein Beat-Kaleidoskop, Europaverlag, Vienna, Austria, 1980.
Over the Stage of Kansas, Telephone Books, NYC, 1973.
The Trashing of America, Cover by Les Levine, Kulchur Foundation, NYC, 1975.
Blue Orchid Numero Uno, Telephone Books, 1977.
Panik in Dodge City, Expanded Media Editions, Bonn, W. Germany, 1981.
Forever Wider, 1954-1984, Scarecrow Press, Metuchen, NJ, 1985.
Was Poe Afraid?, Bogg Publications, Arlington, VA, 1990.

Many of these titles can be found at abebooks.com or alibris.com

Current Titles

Hand on the Doorknob, Water Row Press, Sudbury, MA, 2000
The Last of the Moccasins, Cover by Robert Williams, Mother Road Publications, Albuquerque, NM, 1996.

These titles can be purchased through waterrowbooks.com

Cut Here:A book of recent Plymell collages. This may be purchashed through 12 Gauge Press